Title Page

ISA N WO RU U...
(The Boiling Cauldron)

PRINCE ADEOLA GOLOBA

Dedication

To:

The memory of my dear father, Alhaji (Prince) Yusuf Amuda Yekini Goloba Ashogbon, the Chief Ajagunna of Isolo Kingdom & Borokini Adinni of Ejigbo Central Mosque, and my beloved sisters, Silifah, Sherifah, Shakirah, and Basirah,
who have taken into the air, their final breathe out of
this boiling cauldron and walked into the eternal peaceful Land of our Silent Heroes...

This collection I also dedicate to all the victims of human excesses violently displayed through exploitations, tyranny, oppression, slavery, injustice, evil conspiracies and incessant wars... economic, political, socio-cultural, physical, mental or psychological.

Acknowledgement

First of all, my acknowledgment goes to Olodumare, my maker, designer, and director of my destiny in life. And to every soul with rare human kindness and gift who have given me the reason to believe in the inner gift God has planted in me, and morally, physically, emotionally, mentally and financially urge me to share all of my heartsongs with humanity. I am so grateful and full of thanks, love, appreciations, and respect for you. I am greatly indebted to you all. Amongst you are my dear highly respected beloved and kind, magnanimous, highly intelligent and thorough, father, Big Daddy, teacher, trainer, influencer, Boss and Uncle, an award winning professional Engineer of repute, a man of letters, business mogul and formal President of Awori Welfare Association of Nigeria (AWAN), Chief Solomon Ayinde Ojolowo, The Chief Executive Officer (CEO), S. Ojolowo Technical Company Ltd, a subsidiary of SOT Nig. I most sincerely acknowledge your unquantifiable contributions in my life as a father, you have always been there for me and my family morally, physically, emotionally and financially. I really appreciate you a lot Sir, and I fervently pray that may the Good Lord continue to strengthen and be with you always. My beloved dearest mother, Alhaja Princess Mojisola Aderinsola Goloba Ashogbon (Nee Adebesin) who labored selflessly to care for, defend, protect, provide, love me unconditionally, and instill me, the art of poetry right from childhood, my brothers and Sisters, Prince Akeem Temilade Goloba, Prince

Rasheed Teniola Goloba and his wife Princess Adebimpe Goloba (Nee Oresanya), Princesses Modinat Adenike Sangodele Goloba, Princess Azeezat Adejoke Ehigbor Goloba and my cousin Princess Adepeju Adebesin. Above all, my sincere appreciation goes to my Nephew Prince Adebowale (Anthony) Akeem Goloba Jnr. who always provided me with a lot of technical IT supports during the periods of putting this book together. I am greatly indebted to you for all your moral, mental, emotional and financial supports that you have given to me. My sincere appreciation also goes to my beloved, respected, revered and intelligent brother like father, the Arole Onimewon of our time and the immediate past Head of Fadu Onimewon Royal Family of Ejigbo Awori Lagos State, Prince Olawale Edagbeja, My very profound able, efficient and dynamic Chairman of Ejigbo LCDA, Alhaji Monsuru Oloyede Bello Obe, my dear Brother, our present Head of Family, Alhaji Chief Iskilu Kazeem Awo-Erin, the Asalu of Ejigbo and Ijon Land, Prince Camal Moninuola Rabiu Edagbeja and Prince Alani Rabiu Edagbeja, Prince Kazeem Idowu Abunimase, Prince Saheed Jamiu, Prince Taofeek Ganiu, Alhaji Olohunkemi, Prince Yusuf Amuda Bakare Ibudoosi, Prince Kabiru Yusuf Apaana, Prince Abiodun Goloba, Prince Goloba Obaleke Olohunjuedalo Solihu, and a host of my family members from Fadu Onimewon Royal Family of Ejigbo Awori Lagos State, who always appreciated my arts and also encouraged me through their kind beautiful positive comments on my works and also coming to my rescue through difficult times. I acknowledge the unforgettable positive impacts of my literary teachers, from primary to tertiary institutions, who showed me the road to this beautiful path that I tread today. My appreciation goes to my respected, gifted, profound and beloved Ejigbo High School Literature teacher, Mr. Adebamwi, Prof. Wole Soyinka, Prof. Olu Obafemi, Prof. Femi Osofisan, Prof. Charles Bodunde and Prof. Mahfuz Adedimeji from the Department of English and Foreign Languages, University of Ilorin. I cannot forget the unprecedented influence that the following people have had on me in this journey through the selfless advice, guidance, inspirations and thorough tutelage they have freely offered to me. I have learned, grown and drank from their nectar pots of literary knowledge and wisdom. A poet of international repute and socialist activist, Comrade Aj. Dagga Tolar, the Artistic Director of Aj House of Poetry, and my dear radical cousin, the internationally renowned and Ejigbo born Nigerian award winning Multi-media creative and Visual/performance artist, Prof. Jelili Atiku, who kindly and selflessly used their sleepless nights in editing, revising and re-editing this book till perfection. It would be so unfair and unjust if I fail to acknowledge the inestimable contributions and positive impact the following people have had in my personal and literary journey, the media mogul and culture expert, Jahman Oladejo Anikulapo, artist and cultural advocate, Ayodele Ganiu, Edaoto, Aderemi Adegbite, Princess Adesola Aduke Arit Alamutu, Samuel Osaze, Ozi Okoli, Naza Amaeze Okoli, Prof Akachi Adimora Ezeigbo, Late Prof Jerry Agada, my dear Brother and Boss, Comrade Prince Oluwaseyi Olajide Oyetoro, the Editor-in-Chief of Voice OfAwori

(VOA). You have undoubtedly been my greatest inspiration, and I am so grateful to you all. I must not forget to mention here in appreciation of My indefatigable Comrade and defender of human rights and truth, Comrade Alhaji Jubril Ogundimu and Comrade Afeez Bj Olaleye, Oluwo Oba, who stood by my family till the end when heavy storms of injustice descended on us in Ejigbo. I am so grateful for all of your supports with other members of the Coalition of Oodua Self-Determination Group (COSEG). I pray may God Almighty reward you all abundantly. And finally, my deepest appreciation also goes to so many of you my friends, school and classmates, and my family members and relations that spaces cannot permit me to fill here, I sincerely acknowledge the all of you have one way or the other inspired me in no small measure. I am so blessed to have met them all in my lifetime. And I am so thankful to you all once again for positively inspiring me. I am so grateful to you all and pray that God Almighty bless you and continue to protect you and all your family.

Tennyson's Ulysses at the close of his journey left a resounding and thought-provoking revelation, which will continue to remain indelible in the pages of history. He confessed, "I am a part of all that I have met". In this way, throughout the long voyages of my life, I have come to realise that I could never be divorced from all the countless numbers of people and experiences that I have met with. Therefore, it is my ultimate hope that all of you who have patiently undertaken the journeys in this collection at the end of your journey will never fail to appreciate what you have learnt as a meaningful part of your experience that will complement your understanding of and empathetic concern for all these people for whom the burdens of this life become too great to carry.

Table of Content

Page

Section One

Section Two

Section Three

Preface

It is a part of more than two decades of thematic reflections, which have been painfully conceived and endured that finally gave birth to "ISA N WO RU U...The Boiling Cauldron". Reflections and memories of running years motivated by constant display of violent clash between the tranquil state
of nature and the evil inherent in man, triggered by his selfish lust for sophistication and dominance.

Ours was once a world carved in a perfect harmony, peace and tranquillity, but alas! The sudden emergence of a dangerous civilization with the reign of scientific and technological advancement has come to prove a vulnerable threat to the whole of Humanity and plunge this beautiful world into an endless boiling cauldron…a situation never imagined or experienced by mankind on planet earth.

ISA N WO RU U (Yoruba Language) … subtitled "The Boiling Cauldron" in English Language is a collection of poems gathered in this single carefully thoughtful titled book as a radical response to the socio-cultural, political, economic, environmental, emotional and psychological malaise and injustice perpetrated by man's inhumanity against man. This body of work is created to address the unending issues of fundamental human rights violations unjustifiably committed against harmless innocent individuals and groups of people around the world, especially the children, women, the aged and the physically challenged who have been at the most receiving end of these crimes against humanity. The goal of this piece of work is to share my heartsongs with the world and hope they can relate to it and in turn share with their loved ones, so as to make this world a better place to live.

"ISA N WO RU U...The Boiling Cauldron" is also a body of long bottled heartfelt emotions which have been bubbling for expression for many years, but today, "ISA N WO RU U...The Boiling Cauldron" is finally born, crying so loud against the endless menace of the modern warfare putting the lives of the whole of humanity at stake. Social, economic, political, military, scientific and psychological warfare are such warfare that have characterized genocide, displacements of people from their ancestral Lands and homes, injustice, slavery, exploitation, cruelty and insensitivity to the fundamental rights of fellow man and these have cost them permanent physical, mental and psychological damage.

In other words, "Boiling Cauldron" is a chain of poems in form of lamentations, outright condemnations, stiff resistance and urgent call for a total halt to these unnecessary warfare which have consequently placed too much unbearable burden upon the existence of the whole of humanity. The dehumanizing wound inflicted on the Indigenous Africans by the imperial colonialists are still fresh on our memories; the 1930s holocaust in Germany; the Jewish pogrom in Europe; the Vietnam and the Hiroshima horror! The Bosnian, Sarajevo, Kashmir and the Somalia Nightmares; Delta Storm! Twin Towers, the continuing boiling cauldrons of the Middle - East predicaments, especially in Palestine. Also, at present, mankind is in deep shock and grief as the power brokers of the so called supper powers of the world endlessly clash in war of attrition while Ukraine is being mindlessly ravaged and torn apart by war, and the raging menace of socio-political and ethno-religious violence and the issue of monster terrorism that have refused to leave Nigerian scene through deliberate attempt of ethnic cleansing and genocide, all are constant reminders of the devastating effects of these unjustifiable warfare.

Therefore, it is pertinent to advance at this junction that "warfare cripples human being. Not only does the fury of war disable those who are alive, but it also cuts off the future" *. Hence, all stake holders must rise up now to nail to the ground, this demonic warfare, because mankind no longer can carry the burden of the life draining hot emission from this boiling cauldron.

It is therefore, because of my absolute involvement with humanity and my empathetic concern for the deplorable state of man today that I reckon to the challenge of using this medium to sensitize the modern man towards striking a balance between exercising his God - given intellectual strength over his cosmic environment and his constant relationship with fellow man, so that this world would become a better place to live.

Prince Adeola Goloba

12th December, 2012.

* Edgar V. Roberts: *Writing Themes About Literature* (New Jersey: Prentice Hall Inc. 1964 rpt. 1969, 1973, 1977)p. 128.

<u>Section One</u>

1.   *BOILING CAULDRON*

We came here
To live...in peace
We came…to find love
We aimed…to share our friendship
And hoped…to fully embrace
The cooling breeze of nature.
We sailed, long long distance
From the warmth embrace
Of our mother's womb
To savour the healing scents
Of paradise earth
We came…
To work and tilt the ground
Forever cultivate harmony
On the lush green
Of this globe-like plantation
Alas! We found nothing…
Nothing but strange scurrying bodies
Violently lurking in the shadow
Of the moonlight blaze
Like some turbulent frictions
On extremely hot galaxy
Gold flaming, silver burning
Bronze melting, copper fuming
Ocean surging, global warming
Forest blazing, poisonous air polluting
Earth quaking, flood invading
Power tussling, arms proliferating
Scurrilous rumours spreading, war lingering
Mass weapon destructing, deadly terror striking
Socio-political acrimonies ravaging, ethno-religious struggles consuming
Battles raging, men fighting
Gun shattering, blood shedding
Suicide commissioning, bomb blasting
Love fading, hatred ruling
Peace failing, harmony falling

Hope dying, determination waning
Soul shaking, heart breaking
Aids killing, fear soaring
Hunger maiming, poverty biting
Life's threatened, homes' drenched with chaos
Oh! This place's nothing...but a hot hot zone
Nothing… but a boiling cauldron!

-- 7/11/12
5.30pm
Lagos

2. WEARY WORLD

We are weary world, done with war
Let's live in peace'n'fight no more
No more grudges-let's forget about RACE
'cause our habitat's a global place
Continental curve from Australia, Middle-East to Africa
Asia, through Europe'n'down to America

We're weary world, done with war
We shall live in peace'n'fight no more
No more wars-let's leave not our duties
To cast callous calamity to nature's beauties
Ah! The earth's surface's been defaced
With wars-innocent lives's been displaced

A world are we, totally done with war
In peace shall we live'n'clash no more?
Desert storm at Gulf-Hiroshima! Still flood our memory
Mortal genocide, engineered from bio-atomic nuclear armory
Sarajevo horrors-constant nightmares in Northern Ireland
No peace in Africa-Yet, not one in Switzerland

A world are we, totally done with war
Shall we live now in peace'n'clash no more?
Twin-Towers already've been lost to Terrorism
Million wealth, souls too were sacrificed in horrific barbarism
All these in New-York, West-Bank, Baghdad'n'Kabul
While some missiles passed through Ramala'n'Istanbul

Oh! We're weary world done with war
Let's live in peace'n'quarrel no more
No more wars-Military, Economic or Culture

We've had enough decades of ruthless torture
Kwashiorkor, Tuberculosis, AIDS'n'new born SARS
Imposed by malnutrition, viruses, contagious deadly gas

What is a modern man's fate on earth?
When peace even now has become dearth
We grope for meaningful life-Oh! We cannot see
Our lives've been drown in missiles sea
Let's live in peace now'n'fight no more!
'cause we're a world weary of war

-- 2003
Ilorin

3. THE TROUBLE MAKERS

How our world was carved trouble free,
But, I am troubled with what I see.
Our world've turned to a paradise of war-torn,
This I've known since the time I was born.

We are all thrown in this by trouble-makers,
Who always stage parades as peace-makers,
Let us wake up! Stake-holders!
And together check the excesses of these peace-brokers.

It is the arrogance of men that born tyranny,
Which make them to be guilty of felony.
They carelessly over-stepped their own border,
Executing the agenda of their New World-Order.

With their selfish motives, they invaded our colonies,
They eroded our thoughts, robbed us and make us life's parodies.
They created crisis, wars and broke the still of our nights,
Disguised as peace-makers, they terrorize us with their P-K might.

Crippled-Economy, Social-Anarchy, and Political-Crisis,
Rewards of our loyalties, our deserved prizes.
O peace-makers! We are carcasses of your ravages,
What could we've done to deserve these untold carnages?

As a gift of your foreign policy,
You brought us "Democratic Mobocracy",
Which you've cunningly engineered from the shadow,

And callously launched upon us, this piercing arrow.

You created terror in our lands and make us afraid,
Searching for terrorists, you mercilessly discharge your raid.
In this, I've grown and witness in a daze,
How you've turned our peaceful world to a storming blaze

-- 12/10/02
10.00pm
Lagos

4. MASS ACRE!

Stampede! Wailing! Groaning'n'howling!
Wild cries of nature's gifts tolling
The sky wanderers slowly became dearth
As they dropped to the warmth embrace of mother earth

The sea tricklers no longer make their legendary ripples
Their silences to eternal interment still are riddles
The land dwellers too no more find this place a comfort
As they now lay dead like carcasses, lives devoid of fort.

N...W...O...Terror...Delta-Storm...graves of mass acre!
W...M...D...bombs...September 11, Palestine'n'March 11...
The whole world's submitted to MAD MASSACRE...!

-- 14/3/04
3.00pm
Lagos

5. HOPELESS

Let those who can hear
Stretch their ears to the echoes
Of my groaning voice

Let those who can see
Open wide their eyes to the
Heavy strain in my weary face

And let those who are here today
Be aware that I've been tormented
I may moan to death

Listen to the embittered songs
Of my dying soul, vibrating
All over the universe

Listen to the sonorous songs
Of my innocent'n'helpless soul
Anxiously wished to leave beyond

This soul that has struggled
So much to go beyond, regretted
Living in this place of horror

Here; in this part of the world
Where disregards for humanity prevail
While injustice is paraded as justice

Where man is treated everyday
With unending hatred like a dirty
Ugly animal by fellow man

Where innocent people are harassed
Every now and then; charged
And killed for offences they did not commit

Oh! My sorely soul, weak and tired
Trembling to come back dwell
In this house of horror

For these gory sights haunt...haunt
And gaoled my gentle and noble soul
They are the cause of my torment

But if I offend your sensibilities
Please forgive me for I am gone
The pain is too much for me

Ah! Who will rescue me
From this vein that I languish?
O dearest death! Will you?

The oldest inevitable visitor
Who lived from the beginning of time
And leave no house un-knocked

O death! Come quick!
And knock the door of my soul
I shall open for you; to take me go rest

Let me go; here is not
A better place to live
Let me go...

May be if I go to the world beyond
I may find there in, succour
A noblest endless succour

-- 1998
Lagos

6. ODE TO HUMANITY

How can we make this world a peaceful paradise,
If we don't lay down our arms'n'make simple sacrifice?
And stop this seasonal madness of earthly ravages,

Which've turned us all to carcasses, remnants of such carnages.

Shall we not bury our past and today strive for unity?
So that tomorrow, in tranquillity we live, till eternity.
Shan't we flush out the venomous contents of our blood,
Which always surge like deadly temper of Babylonian flood?

Ah! Terrorism! The monster neo-god is in our midst,
But…where did he coast from to launch his fearful fist?
These threat of war, terror'n'horror that envelop our earth,
When shall we harvest them all out of our heart?

O sunshine! You must rise and melt assunder!
This constant baffling roar of saddening thunder,
Or innocent grasses shall always lie beneath the careless
pleasures,
Of two giant elephants, locking horns'n'trampling life's treasures.

How? How can we make this world a peaceful paradise,
If we don't lay down our arms'n'make simple sacrifice?
O poets! Arise! You've great burdens upon you to bear,
And your pens, your songs, can always pierce away our fear.

-- 2003
Ilorin

I DON'T EVEN KNOW WHAT TO DO

I don't even know what to do
Just like I know not what to say

To the war that looms here everyday
Oh! How can I ever share this with you?

How can I ever share this with you?
When you move far away in thoughts from me
But how do you take these ruins to be?
Oh! I don't even know what to do

Just like I know not what to say
To the waste of life's treasures every night'n'day
Like desert carcasses, bodies float here'n'there
Oh! How else can I make you all aware?

How else can I make you all aware?
That we all have great burdens upon us to bear
Mothers,children,howling to death from nuclear spray
Oh! From the war that looms here everyday

From the war that looms here everyday
You gain; you find pleasures in laying harms
Since you don't want to lay down your arms
What can I do now or say...?

-- 2002
Ilorin

8. TO THE LAST

Artilleries?
What are these in our cities?
Is this another season I've always known?

Or another festival of game hunting?
These faces I've always known,
Carrying murderous massive artilleries,
Tracking us to death as their preys or quarries,
Displacing us away from our father's shelters,
Our properties, our treasures, they always cart away.
Alas! We're helpless…but we shall fight,
fight against this encroachment,
To the last against these Brito-American night marauders.
But why do they come to slaughter and ravage?
What could we've done to deserve such carnage?
They always tell us that they are liberators,
But with all these artilleries, are they not dictators?

-- 13/3/03
11.00pm
Ilorin

9.   *CEASELESS*

I do not know when these will end,
Destructions with which our hands we make
Confusions, wars'n'hatred that we cannot tend
Senseless civilization! Putting our lives at stake.

Yea! I know, someday, these nonsense'd cease,
When we shall've the cooling mercy of peaceful breeze.

-- 2001
Ilorin

10. TILL WE HEAL

Our hearts you must know always bleed,
Because of your aggressive prejudise'n'greed.

Our anger we must say always flood,
Because you let our bodies flow in our blood.

Revenge in our hearts will cease not to loom,
Because you've set for us our doom.

Our hearts always will bleed,
If you do not end the hatred you've breed.

Why do their hearts bleed they ask?
But they know they've wounded our hearts with axe.

Ha! America! You stormed our land, drained our soil,
In Palestine, Middle-East, you maimed our life-toil.

You all like vultures gather'n'hover around,
Always upon where images like carcasses abound.

Rest? Your minds never shall embrace but ills
You'n'your morrows, till the wound in our hearts heals.

-- 12/4/03
2.25am
Ilorin

11. PENITENCE

These scars I carry now,
No, is not of nature,
But that marked long ago
By some strange greedy scavengers
Is it my inadequacy that
Here as Black, I gabble?
You say 'am backward now
Burdened with ugly civil unrests,
Born by your cunny incursions
Into these my mangled territories,
Devouring my values, as crows

Vultures'n'hawks do to carrions.
Now I grimace with constant palpitations
From horrible nightmares of wallowing
In the oases of neo-colonialism,
Gnawing at my future;Africa!
Gloomy indeed tomorrow thus appears,
But that your incisive mind
Can make those greedy scavengers
Pay back for these in penitence…

-- 2003
Ilorin

12. I NEVER KNEW…

I never knew that it was the man
That by the river bank stood beside the ban

Until the plague my inner sense uncover
From my mind, my brain and my eyes then I discover
Staring endlessly in happy and careful observation
The deadly job our puppet brothers got with compensation
Wilfully demonstrated by the first son of our mother's torture
Against the physical structure of our mother's nature.

Wither my offspring? Mother's mourning helplessly?
As our brothers drag on endlessly
Our mother along in the river with violent strangulation
When some of us children slowly submit to starvation
Some of us even fight and innocently kill one another
Not knowing that it was the man that always calls an order.

-- 20/11/2000
11.00pm
Lagos

13. DREADED OWLS

This is the face of the monsters!
As ugly as dreaded owls
plying from the cities abroad
And landing on our coast's shore
Glowing with beautiful green pasture
That always feed that flamboyant innocent cow
Which comfortably and peacefully breeds
Breeds and breeds in millions
Do you gentle goddess of the pasture
Ever know hunger through your years?
For there were sweet green for you to swallow

Pure spring to gulp
And free fresh breeze to bathe
Until they come and choke you

This is the face of the monster!
Who have come to enslave you
On your back landed they endless whips
Yet they persist not in sucking
Your breast with cunny greediness
They suck and suck your breasts
Without mercy under duress
So that you become lean
Like a pair of a palm-broom
And you swerve left and right
By the force of a gentle little wind
Which've come your way
And travelled through the west
From the ancient horizon.

This is the face of the monster!
Whom by the terror they unleash upon you
You groan'n'moan in silence
In gnawing pain, you ceaselessly slump
And wail bitterly for your children
For there are no more green

For them to swallow
No more spring to gulp
And the nature's breeze
Is no more healthy to wallow in
Yet they never stop to suck your sweet breasts
Unless if wonders prevail
I wonder if you could ever be let go
Now that you're bowing to mother earth.

-- 21/11/2000
6.00am

Lagos

14. A TIME SO LONG

Arise Africa!
For too long you've slumbered.
Africa arise!
Too many days have gone by
But all was too hard
Too tough a time.

Arise Africa!
Yesterday was a time
A time so long and too hard for you
Millions of years have become yesterday
But all was too hard
Too tough a time for you

Arise Africa!
Today has come
And yet another time
And yet another time

Another time that will become yesterday
O mother Nation! Wrestle hard and never you give up!
For I don't know where today is leading to

But arise Africa!
For too long you've slumbered
And want me not the repeat of yesterday
For millions of tomorrow will soon become yet another yesterday
Arise mother Nation!
And let me see where tomorrow will lead you to.

-- 1999
Lagos

15. ODE TO A POWER PLAYER

O infamous power player! Threading boastfully on a dreaded path,
A path so fragile, even for great warriors to pass.
O power player! Thou ski roughly down a dangerous slope,
Where the skilled skiers go on a careful rope.
O foster child of fortune! Sitting majestically on a mortar pavement
Completely possessed with whips for fellow mortals punishment.
But upon me, softly...softly...I say, mine pleading message to thee,
To breath the gentle air of mercy like an early morning's dew.
O threashous power player! Careful! Thou must be careful!
For power! Yes power! Could drive thee like a fool.
Power! Yes, I say power! Could intoxicate,
And make thee its victim: then veer like a carriage,
Manoeuvred by a drunken driver and stagger,
Like a man who has had one bottle too much over.
Over and over, thou could finally land in a ditch,
And no one would ever be there and free to give you a lift.
O dearest power player! Fair! Is the caution; fair play!
The harbinger of the needed justice, in clear day.
And never thou try, O power player! To be a poor player!
To risk thee down into a shameful danger.

-- 1998

Lagos

16. *LAST NIGHT*

Last Night,
I saw many poets, mourning;
Mourning the fall, the fall
Of another poet,
Crushed down at Ikoyi,
By the buzzing rockets
Of the State's Agents,
The epitome of mortal's destruction,
That sends him down
Under his tombstone, hidden;
And recalling late memories of the present gone
From the epitaph within
With gold written lines.

My sense numb and plague,
By their screaming car and laughter,
Oscillating up and down
Their used apparatus in triumph.
And speeding off fast and disappear
Into the invisible darkness of the night.
And the soul of the poet's dead and gone.
And this one poet,
Horror! Horror! Gasped,
And sinks to the ground, groaning
Shedding blood and ocean
And wail, like cherubim in brunt
For the wasted spirit of a dear friend

The Poet!

-- 2001
Lagos

17. *RED SURFACE*

Wailing wounds! Wailing wounds!
Will time have you undo?
The wounds are wailing
Wailing like thunder from the great river's waves
For the great indelible age-mark of inflictions
Abandoned by the mortal son of antagonism

Wailing wounds! Wailing wounds!
Will time have you undo?
Red on your surface
Written boldly like blood-paints
On the moon's surface
Wailing wounds! Will time have you undo?

Wailing wounds! Wailing wounds!
Will time have you undo?
When your right heart is drowned
Drowned and wailed for justice
Red on your surface! Wailing wounds!
Will time have you undo?

Wailing wounds! Wailing wounds!
There is Red on your surface
If the past is naked
And sailed to the present
As if to bid vengeance
Wailing wounds! Will time have you undo?

Wailing wounds! Wailing wounds!

Red on your surface; wailing…
       Wailing like thunder from the great river's waves
     For the great indelible age-mark of inflictions
   Abandoned by the mortal sons of antagonism
Wailing wounds! Will time have you undo?

-- 2000
Lagos

18. CHAOS

Africa! Ah! In disarray, every morning I worry.
Our household is falling in helpless state of sorry.
Wars; like bride'n'groom we marry.
Guns, canisters, ballistic missiles'n'mines we now carry.
Every day, paa! Paa! Paa! We take cover in a hurry.
Kinsmen wailing…around their corpses, they scurry.
Every night's a bitter nightmare, blood sights are gory.
Our ancestors legacies, all now dead'n'packed in a lorry.
Let's stop these senseless killings, live in peace'n' not tarry.
While external forces, we should join hands together to parry.

-- 2003
Ilorin

19. OUR TALES

From many seasons of carnage
We have grown to be like a clan of savage

Why do we always go on rampage
To slaughter ourselves and ravage?

Every cock-crow at dawn
Horror wakes us but to strikes us down

We cannot go to sleep without fear and cries
By twilight when the whole clan crumbles and lies

Kinsmen of Ijaw! O Itsekiri brothers!
If you care not, Mother Earth bothers!

Because we roast our own folks to ashes
Mother Nature whips us with painful lashes

Ife-Modakeke struggle must yield to lasting tame
Aerewa-Afenifere discord must become permanent lame

Bakasi Boys...Boko Haram! Please…you must go to rest
Lay down your arms like O.P.C. in the West

No more pastoral or Imamate clashes
Guard yourself from political rashes

But why do we always go on rampage
To slaughter ourselves and ravage?

Fight over oil, land or some sacred cake
Seized by some modicum scrooge to rake?

We have heads but cannot think
Water we possess but cannot drink

Enough food but still rage on with hunger
No wonder we always let loose with anger

We have shelter but no place to hide
While we run helter-skelter when we take side

Storming with vengeance like maddening flood
Here lie our body in boiling pools of blood

Ah! We have life…we cannot live
But when shall all these strives finally take leave?

Our home is burning…Oh where do we go?
Everywhere is already set aglow

From North, East, West and Southern zones
Across the plains echoed the clinging of our bones

Endless strives…what did we gain?
Save mourning, cries of woes and pain

Shall we not end these seasons of carnage?
And cease to be like a clan of savage?

Come together to clear our ravages
And move to undone the damages

Call on God to send down His Merciful Aids
And save us from untold wanton and A.I.D.S

God Please! Send down your soothing rain!
To come cool and wash away our burning pain

Calm our anger and rages
And make us again like old sages

Give us profitable life
Let us live like true brothers…free us from strife

Give us beautiful places here to hide
And let our space be wide

Let all stakeholders sow love and not tarry
Upon greed and hatred that we now carry

Like a phoenix rebuild our nation
And let each clan harvest its ration

No more rampages
Nor slaughter and ravages

Let us end these seasons of carnage
And cease to be like a clan of savage

What legends shall be left for the unborn
When we go yonder and leave the stage to burn?

What chants will roll on their tongues
When they come to behold our wrongs?

Brothers! If we end not these seasons of carnage
And cease to be like a clan of savage

Our tales shall be like that "Ballad of Rage"
Told from the first to the very last historical page.

-- 15/12/11
3.40am
Lagos

20. *A PLEA FOR LOVE*

Let there be love, Brothers!
Let there be unity, Nations!
Let peace be reign,
And make this planet
A peaceful paradise.

With love, we are created.
With unity, the sun and the moon,
Discharges their responsibilities.
And with peace, the whole universe,
Does not collapse.

Though we have differences,
Never…never must we forget those differences,
But recognize and respect them,
Respect them, so that
We can live in peace.

Let us not live in hatred.
Let us all come together,
And do things in common,
Like the sun and the moon.
Let us not destroy this beautiful world with war.

So Brothers! Nations! Let there be true love,
And unity of purpose for all of us to reach,
The peak of the highest mountain,
And live forever in peace on this planet,
Until death do us part

-- 1999
Lagos

<u>Section Two</u>

1. *WHERE ARE THEY?*

Where are our glories?
Where are they?
Where are the glories of our fathers?
The glories won by the great achievements
Of our great Nationalists.
Where are the glories of our Land?
The prides of our Nation.
The prides of our great Grand-fathers.
Our prides, our glories, where are they?
They are lost and carved away by the ugly ones.

The precious glories of our Land,
Are nowhere to be found.
The glories that gloweth and extended
To the North, South, East and the Western zones.
The glories that shineth from the horizon,
And embodied the whole land of our fathers.
These glories, our glories, are nowhere to be found.
For the ugly ones are not yet dead,
Yet, the beautiful ones are not yet born,
To return the lost glories of our glorious Land.

-- 1997
Lagos

2   FAKE PHYSICIAN

We always think you as good politicians
But failed to see you as fake physicians

You numb our senses, claim to be our Sheppard
But wait! You're still the same Leopard

Away with you! Sons of that cursed *Leper*
Bite like some witches, spirits or some kind of viper

You think us as just mundane
So you treat us with such obvious disdain

Your claims are full of double-senses, intentions nefarious
Never again shall we believe in lies so contagious

You break our hearts…dash our hopes with such lesions
Our beautiful homes now are filled with great tensions

Alas! You shall answer…PAY the PRICE from GENESIS
That's the call from the ancient god called NEMESIS

-- 28/5/09
10.25am
Lagos

3. FUTILITY

Futility! All in futility!
When thy little sojourn spent seemed infinity
Mine blazing hope away freeze 'n' melt to eternity
When thy provoke mine fiery zeal with all insanity
By a million sweet promises made in reality
Mine moments shoot 'n' away shrank without fertility
If thou rest upon man thy soul in totality
Always'll man've thee crash in futility

Even as thy apparition drawn near in mine false sensibility
In vanity hath mine self land to true visibility
And like deserts be mine zeal in futility
O rest not thy soul upon man in totality
*But only *CHI* alone thou should upon lay thy morality*
Even as will man cease not to sail through mortality.

-- 2001
Ilorin

4. BETRAYAL

A b-r-o-k-e-n heart
Is like a q...u...a...k...e... earth
When joy's suddenly dethroned for sorrow
It pains deep to the marrow.

The heart t-r-e-m-b-l-e-s
But earth r...u...m...b...l...e...s...
At the slightest storm of a saddening thunder
Which makes the whole world to s-c-a-t-t-e-r
a...s...u...n...d...e...r...

When trust, hope or love's betrayed
The chance of a new morrow's quickly allayed
The mind then'll be dangerously left docile
And the bones no more will become agile

B-r-o-k-e-n heart! Where is thy true friend?
That will come to thee now'n'mend
And bring thy unfailed hope in haste
That thou shall not become a waste.

-- 2/1/04
7.05pm
Lagos

5. SOLITUDE

Seek not thy joy in solitude,
Far beyond…there lies in magnitude,
Endless pang of living pains…
That storms the heart and reigns…

If thou seek a splendours life,
And not venture in lifeless strife.
Seek thou in nature's perfect path,
But not in solitude's painful wrath.

Solitude! Solitude! Life's greatest foe,
Count me not the object of thy woe.
As thou seek a friend in me,
Oh! Thy plot never shall live to be.

Even though, this world's turned to rumble,
And no more life dwells in this once a beautiful jungle.
But count me not the object of thy woe,
Solitude! For thou art the life's greatest foe.

-- 2004
Ilorin

6. MEMORIES…

I've never uncovered through the passages of time,
Why my wandering thought refused to find a rhyme,
With many realities of life since my prime,
Not even when I finally discovered myself to be a clime.

I've locked horn together through history with lingering memories,
To unravel why our lives are inevitably curled around strange mysteries,
Oh! The mystical memories of onsavouring the genesis of social maladies,
Still; memories, which come and go, as nightingales, full of soothing
melodies.

I've wandered in the wilderness of my lustful thoughts,
Crossing through painful moments of turbulent drought,
Which WE weary sons of helpless but suffering mortals are caught,
Deep in the cold dungeon of THEIR plot.

I've relived from the romantic room of my passionate breast,
Great vision of the birth-time of my ageing quest,
When sufferings'n'sorrows, hostilities'n'hatred shall pass beyond to rest,
For beautiful and wonderful memories, once more to gain, eternal conquest.

I've finally arrived from the journey through "THE COLD MOONS",
Where the "WHEELS" of fate betray life too soon,
With new memories of hope, love, peace'n'tranquility, forever clung to heart,
As Oak-Tree does, to the warmth embrace of mother earth.

-- 2002
Ilorin

7. GONE IS THE GLORY OF THE YORE

Gone is the glory of the yore
Lost was her streaming blessing that always pour
When Academics was once a marvellous tour
Today! Oh! I am completely ruled by sorrow
Very bleak, dim, honestly seem be my morrow
See how my heart aches and strained be my marrow
No doubt! I sure you shall have me pity
If you burrow thus deep down my city

To witness the gory storm's gravity
 I suffer from recurrent insomnia; Oh! I cannot sleep
 For insolent generations have our campuses creep
 Always celebrating seasons of lethal storms to've terror reap
 O once upon a paradise of wisdoms to crave

 Where generations of the fore learned with brave
 Here now, is the dungeon of hell, our grave
 Where we live and groan in Academic leprosy
 Moral'n'intellectual tumor, psychological lesion strikes by proxy
 No! No more wits like possessed the fore brains
 Only Sadism! Sadism! Reigns with her thorn chronic strains
 We've been plagued on our campuses with sudden rages
 Hunted every time, down to death, and they're gone our sages
 We've been sieged under new colonial cages
 And in the hands of the safarians, we've become preys of their wages
 O beloveth glory of the fore! Now that we grope in silence for
freedom
 Will you ever return to have us back our wisdom?

-- 2/10/01
6.30am
Ilorin

8. FAMILIAR SENSATIONS

 Oh Nemesis it is!
 What are these? Am I dreaming?
 What apparitions plunge my skull
 To constriction?

 My mind's vision
 My power will to cease?
 By murderers! Ferocious, foreign,
 And familiar sensations!
 Like hired assassins!

Oh Nemesis it is!
Our home is crashing
Under the yoke
    Of borrowed civilizations;
    Atheism! Alcoholism!
Paganism, promiscuity and hooliganism!

    While our masters
Plunder on our treasury,
There is war everywhere.
        And the rest of us
Wallow in poverty,
And dine with hunger,
        Our indispensable mortal enemy.

    Aids too, crept in silently,
Like thieves to horrify our lives
With non-atonable demands.
        And all our manpower
        Are dropping dead,
By the menace of these dreaded gods
That must be worshipped,
        With sacrifices every seasons.

    Oh Nemesis, it is!
 Alas! Our future is nothing but bleak
 Bleak but thin…
        And there is no known hope
 To lean on…
 Except to remember,
        And turn back to pay homage,
        To the willful will,
 Of our forgotten Master.

-- 12/6/01
2.45pm
Lagos

9. TEMPEST

It all came like in a dream,
    Thunderous roar of a strange storm's stream.

Strange cries of birds across the sky,
Helter-skelter, wither they fly?
Cloud overshadowed, heaven ridiculed,
By the saddening temper of earthly particles,
Which overthrow the air with massive pressure,
Causing callous end to life's treasures beyond measure,
Deafening smash of window panes from wind-flood,
Surging deep into men's flesh to split their blood.
Others cried'n'raced away from a dreadful draught,
Away to refuge, before the looming doom's brought.
Hey! What here now? No refuge against darkness storm,
Accompanied by thunderbolt, rainstorm that turned this city to
slum.

-- 22/3/03
11.45pm
Ilorin

10. SLOWLY
(To Mama & sibling)

Life's a struggle…
's the reason why we must always hustle
From Mama's womb'n'deep down to the grave
But… triumph is only to the brave
Who trudge on'n'not let WILL fade
On slowly…on the wheels of life's fate.

-- 30/10/03
2.55pm

Lagos

-- 9/7/06

11. SLEEPLESS

Why can't I every night go to sleep
When the whole worlds are busy snoring deep?
Why do I battle with restlessness
Each night I am steep in sleeplessness?
Why can't I lie down and rest
But keep scanning my head and breast?
O sleeplessness! Why? whyyyyy?
I'd break down and cry
Why do you always come to haunt
The time I am to climb the snoring mount?
What charge hath thou against me?
Tell me now! Or you let me be!
Come…come please, come now if you know
And help me out of this caustic blow

-- 9/7/06

4.25am
Lagos

12. MIDNIGHT RAPE

Every night that I lay upon my bed
Snoring deep like a dead
They come suddenly'n'murder my sleep
Altering my dreams I wake up'n'weep

Rattling, struggling, dragging, Rats plunder my stock
Bed-bugs, mosquitoes prey upon my blood'n'suck

Small cockroaches too invade'n'*Tambolo* will bite
For blood-suckers, before dawn're all out of sight

Why they come at such a time I snore deep
I do not know, but their menace'll make me weep
Even I cannot my sweet dreams hold'n'save
Coz every time of my night's a midnight rape...

-- 5/5/03
3.30am
Ilorin

13. MAROKO

Steeped deep in slumber; I fearfully nimble on…
On waddling along a sloppy slum,
Like a black lonely weary duck,
Caught amidst a deafening thunderstorm,
Dropping pellets of silver stones
Down sliding through Celestial Doors
A sudden call to halt earthly devotions
Market closing, helter-skelter, people now run
Right into those suspended huts at Maroko
Dogs barking, cocks crowing, birds crying
Dry earth turns sudden flood
Because Mother Nature is at work

Oh! It's thunderstorm! That wakes me up
And save me from this frightening dream…

-- 2003
Lagos

14. OJI RIVER

Our sights were blind with horror!
On a day Chimaroke roads unleashed their terror
A day Nnamani highways were seriously hungry
Was a day Oji River was so angry

Sacrifice! Sacrifice! Oji River wailed in rumble
As the roads' agents went awild in open jungle
To strangle down the helpless scape-goats
For the Mighty Lord of Nsukka roads

How can we appease the power that be?
To calm the angry spirit of this Sea
That has drained travellers' blood on Sunday night
When THE YOUNG…IFESINACHI took off their flight

On a August Sunday were they rubbled down
That 24th night at ENUGU before dawn
Ah! This was a day Oji River was so angry
Because Onitsha highways were seriously hungry.

-- 2003
Lagos

15. SUNDAY DOOM

Ah! Another day of reckoning!
Not realizing it, was beckoning…
When in Lagos we were steeped in deep slumber,
And left upon the laughing sun our bomber,
And then bursted in anger'n'brought upon us, our Sunday doom,
What follows were the destructions that suddenly zoom.

When lives, properties, in seconds were callously wasted,
Our stronghold, powerhouse, our precious hopes're humbly roasted.
Like ashes, they've all gone back to mother soil,
All the million years of our straining toil.

And like the day of Armageddon, Red again in murderous motion,
All our mortal wealths were buried n Canal Ocean.
Perpetrated by incontinental ballistic missiles' deliveries,

Which is the horror, the fruit of our modern day discoveries.
Oh! My life's done! What is the next line of action?
Because I cannot myself unravel this mythical friction.

-- 28/01/02
6.05pm
Ilorin

16. WHEN DARKNESS STORMS

When darkness storms
Then, the light is gone
When the light is gone
Then, darkness shall storm
When the ocean is dry
Unto the air the fishes breathe their last
Oh! When tragedy is done!
Then great sorrow shall fall

When death finally storms
And the soul is suddenly struck
Then tragedy is already done
Oh Death! Oh Death!
Thy beholder of tragedy
Upon us, you've descended
Your blanket of darkness
And Hamzah… now is no more!

-- 22/12/01

12.45pm
Ilorin

17. ODE TO SHERIFAH

Oh! How can I forget my dearest so fast?
When I never thought those moments to last
The joys 'n' laughter of our glorious childhood
When mother 'n' father still laboured for our livelihood
Ooh! Your sudden exit's a painful dagger in my heart
When I never heard the call of the mother earth
No! I was too innocent! Too innocent to know!
That it was the time when the west –wind doth blow
You closed your eyes 'n' I thought you were sleeping
Not knowing that you'll never wake up breathing
On the last day I saw you slept
I had a terrible dream, at your tombstone I wept
A terrible dream on the day my sister died,
All the heavens 'n' earths utterly went awild.
And the glowing sky went sober 'n' looked ugly,
Groaning, moaning, howling, she echoed loudly.
Only for her, the precious lost, she wailed bitterly,
And the earth too was soaked 'n' shivered silently.
0 Sherifah! How can I forget you too soon?
When you always appear to me on the moon

Reminding me of the day you laid to rest
But I know I shall always be your very best
When soon, I am there together with you in bliss
So sleep! Sleep soundly my dear, forever in peace!

-- 3/9/02
3.17am
Ilorin

18. ADIEU...SHAKIRAH

Now that you go down 'n' sink
Eat whatever they eat there 'n' drink what they drink
We already know that death'd be our final fate
What we do not know is when we shall be late

Adieu! Shakirah Adieu! Your sisters're waiting
While we stay here all days mourning 'n' wailing
Tell Zulfah, that with tears in our eyes
And sherifah, that in our memories their fall always lies

Today, ah! Your sisters've gone
We know by tomorrow, our lives too'll be done
Adieu! I bid you peace till we hear the bell
Adieu! Go rest! Only time will finally tell.

-- 23/4/03
2.35am
Ilorin

19. NIGH FALL AT DAWN

Rainfall… nightfall at dawn
Oh! Shuaib! To wherever've you been drawn?

Ah! The Crescent've grown 'n' your Sun's set
And now! The green lawn's been wet

At day-break, we woke up 'n' see you're no more
Ah! Yunus! Our hearts've gone sore

How come you go dwell under soil?
And wait not to taste the fruits of your toil

All you've done here is like a mount'
But CRESCENTERS shall never fail to count

Know that your struggles shall never be in vain
What you've left behind will continue to reign

Today; all your dreams've been torn
May be tomorrow, a new Crescent will be born

Go in peace 'n' step thy tomb'th your right sole
Allah subuhanahu wata'lah will keep your soul

It's rainfall…nightfall at dawn

Adieu! Our rare gem…as you go down

-- 2003
Ilorin

20. ODE ON A FALLING STONE
(To Segun Olusola)

O Death!
Thou art the agent of mystery
Oh! You've struck again!
You strangulate my soul every second
And like a jailbird you doped it
Down your master's dungeon permanence
Is this a mandate fun?
Aren't you jaded?
No wonder, thou art the spirit
Of the underworld
That stole Abacha away yesterday
But how you broke into Aso-Rock
I do not know
It is a puzzle to me
How you captured M.K,O, Kudirat, Funsho
And Yaradua into the world beyond
Many have you seized
With your cold iron grip
Now, you've struck again,
O manipulated agent of mystery!
You've malevolently thrashed Giwa, Fella
And Stella into a palace of no return
And carelessly dragged away Solarin, Wiwa
And Loco, and Clarus, and igbokwe,
Dagrin and Yekini into the land
Of our Silent Heroes

Now, you've come for me
But wait…I must know now
Where you camp the noble spirits
Of our falling Stars
Before I drop
Thou cruel mortal's tyrant
Here I jauntily stand
And do not afraid of you anymore
For I know, I shall journey
A permanent temporal rest
But the day I rise
Thou shall be permanently lampooned
To the death…and I shall forever live
In time's timeless space

-- 6/10/12
7.05pm
Lagos

<u>Section Three</u>

1. *WHERE IS THY ROYAL STAFF?*

O Royal Sky! Where is thy Royal Staff?
Thy whole body is overcast and move around,
All days, all nights,
Thy face is dark.
Thy look ugly as if to cry,
And throw down the Royal Staff

In all the villages, the lands are dead
All the crops, fruits and the trees are dying.
The farms are empty
And all the animals are thirsty
The people in the villages
Everyone are starving

Where is thy Royal Staff?
To wake the dead lands
To wet the drying crops, fruits and trees
To fill the empty farms
And quench the animals of their thirst
And to revive the starving people

Sometimes we love to see you
When looking beautiful and smiling
Because we are comfortable
Sometimes we hate to see you
When looking beautiful and smiling
Because comfortable we feel not

And when looking ugly and crying
Do we love to see you
Because we are comfortable
And while looking ugly and crying
Do we really hate to see you
Because comfortable we feel not

Now...We are happy to see you!
Looking Ugly; but thou never cry
What is the cause? O Royal Staff!
Hath thou lost thy Staff?
Or thou hold it up there in anger?
O Royal Staff! Cry...and throw down thy Royal Staff!

-- 1997
Lagos

2.   *RECKONING*

When men is in trouble,
To scale through, they struggle.

When the animals face battle,
To save face they rattle.

When the ocean weather became turble,
All the trickling fishes will no more bustle.

And when the Soldier Ants encounter bridle,
They withdraw and quickly fizzle.

The day of reckoning thus epitomize beyond these sample,
Where man will finally assemble.

Before their maker shall they stand in humble,
And they shall be left alone in fuddle

Only those who to His Will, submit and struggle,
Shall forever in paradise dwell and be Noble.

-- 2000
Lagos

3.   *PARADOX*

Life? What is life?
How can I ever know what life is?
The life I know, yes! The life
I know is everything,
Everything, so full of paradox.

The life I know is a chameleon,
Bringing different colours all time
The life I know is dynamic, like
The moon'n'the sun moving from the East
To the West'n'from the West to the East.

The life I know is the time,
Bringing forth Day'n'Night
And bringing forth Night'n'Day.
The life I know is the pendulum.
Dangling Left'n'Right and Right'n'Left

The life I know is the bodies,
Orbiting the nucleus,
Without a minute stop.
Can anything stop the movement?
No! Never never can it be stopped.

The life I know is more than these,
Everything, so full of paradox.
The life I know is to create'n'destroy,
And to destroy'n'create,
The life I know is more than these.

The life I know is more than these,
Everything, so full of paradox.

The life I know is to live'n'die,
And to die'n'live,
The life I know is more than these.

The life I know is more than these,
Everything, so full of paradox.
The life I know is to succeed'n'fail,
And to fail'n'succeed,
The life I know is more than these.

The life I know is more than these,
Everything, so full of paradox.
The life I know is to meet'n'miss,
And to miss'n'meet.
The life I know is more than these.

The life I know is more than these,
Everything, so full of paradox.
The life I know is to love'n'hate,
And to hate'n'love.
The life I know is more than these.

The life I know is more than these,
Everything, so full of paradox.
The life I know is to give'n'take,
And to take'n'give.
The life I know is more than these.

The life I know is more than these,
Everything, so full of paradox.
The life I know is to rejoice'n'be sad
And to be sad'n'rejoice,

The life I know is more than these.

The life I know is more than these,
Everything, so full of paradox.
    The life I know is to be heal'n'be ill,
And to be ill'n'be heal.
    The life I know is more than these.

    The life I know is more than these,
Everything, so full of paradox.
    The life I know is to cry'n'laugh,
And to laugh'n'cry.
    The life I know is more than these

    The life I know is more than these,
Everything, between dream'n'reality,
        And between reality'n'dream.
The life I know is far far more than these,
        Everything, so full of paradox.

-- 1997
Lagos

4.   EVERY CLAY

Every Clay, like the sun rise'n'set each passing day,
Will go on waking'n'sleeping this very way.
And like pendulum clock calls to suddenly stay,

So shall every Clay be put to final lay?

-- 2001
Ilorin.

5.   *THESE UNBREAKABLE*

Sojourns! Great Sojourns!
Wanderers! Noble travellers!
The most exclusive sailors
Of this ancient Universe.

Chains of families; round your neck
Locked at your wrists; and your ankles
Of friends; tied and encircled round
Your own physical structure

These unbreakable chains of wealth
Put there by a powerful
Invisible element

Hurray! It's time to go
For you've reached the crossroad
Time! Is drawing! Drawing near
Like a setting sun

But when it is time to go
The unbreakable; will break and cut off
For you have to go
Your destination way

When it is time to go
The great sojourns
Shall never want to leave behind
The unbreakable chains
Put there by a powerful
Invisible element

Oh! Time is drawing! Drawing near
Like a setting sun
But when it is time to go
The unbreakable; will break and cut off
For you have to go
Your destination way

When it is time to go
These noble wanderers
Would fight hard
Never to lose
All their acquired wealth

Oh! Time is drawing! Drawing near
Like a setting sun
But when it is time to go
The unbreakable; will break and cut off
For you have to go
Your destination way.

When it is time to go
These travellers
Would fall in total sorrowness
To part away
From their noble families

Oh! Time is drawing! Drawing near
Like a setting sun
But when it is time to go
The unbreakable; will break and cut off
For you have to go
Your destination way.

When it is time to go
The adventurers; heartbroken
Will shed; basket full of tears
To miss forever, their best friends
For they never wish to say
Good-bye…to their loved ones

Oh! Time is death'n'death is time
But when it is time to go
The cock would crow
The trumpet will blow
And death shall descends
Like a sunset

And the unbreakable; will break and cut off
For you have to go
Your destination way.

-- 3/10/99
2.03am
Lagos

6.   *TO THE SOUND OF SILENCE*

Lest I was a lonely man
On a winter night, I was lost…
To the sound of silence
Alas! Braaa! Baamm! Came the most
Unexpected explosion of a century
It caused my teenage heart
Into a sudden and terrible shock
And almost torn it apart
Then I was forcefully dragged

Out of that world of loneliness

Lest I was a lonely man
When that strange blast of the powerful thunder
Came with the emergence
Of an eye-blinded ray of lightning
It came like the dreadful sound of a volcano
It came like the blast of that Big Bang!
Of which my old grand-teacher told of
And my natural drum
Was almost put asunder.

Lest I was a lonely man
When the sharp ray of lightning
Came and fizzled away in a flash
It came like an explicit display
Of divine Revelation that:
This world was not my home
It came like a vision and made me to see clearly
That only a traveller and stranger am I
 A wanderer and adventurer
On this empty and deceitful planet.

Lest I was a lonely man
When it finally dawn on me
That adequately would it be of me
Never to perpetrate any atom
Of grossly anti-natural exhibits
Upon this temporal world of luxuries
For one day and one second
Would a sudden end come upon me
And I inevitably would be committed to this

Lonely and hungry mother earth for breakfast, lunch or
dinner.

 Lest I was a lonely man

Did I have the knowledge that
If no adequacy is not unidentified with me
Upon this Romantic World
Here then! May I be locked in indefinite loneliness
Here! May I dwell in lonely sufferness
In lonely wilderness may I be
Under this lonely barricade
And here! May I be in lonely torture
For no definite time.

-- 1999
Lagos

7.   WILDERNESS

You my friend! Who is burdened with soberness.
You! Who have lost into the desert of loneliness.
You! Who with your chin on your palm,
Your elbow on your lap,
Your feet on the floor,
Rain down endless tears
From your heavily clouded lids
And strained face.
Groaning faintly like a little lad,
Who has lost his mother

You have toiled on the land,
And on the sea, you have suffered.
You have travelled far and wide,

And wandered in the wilderness.
What strain and pain have you not experienced?
What lost, failure and sorrow
Have you not nurtured on the bed of your heart?
You have wandered in the wilderness!

But your thought is dangerously at climax!
Would thou not commit self-immolation?
What is the matter with you?
What worry has haunted you?
And what mares have gloomed your reasoning?
To make you lose your sense
Of awareness of your forest of God.
What has saddled and clouded your thought?
To make you forget,
That no mortal shall exit
Under this sky's mysterious beauty,
Without wearily wandering
In his own forest of God.
A calculated Will from the owner of the forest.

Remember! You my friend! Who is burdened with
soberness.
You! Who have lost into the desert of loneliness.
You! Who with your chin on your palm,

Your elbow on your lap,
Your feet on the floor,
Rain down endless tears,
From your heavily clouded lids
And strained face.
All is not but lost!
Patience! Endurance! Faith and perseverance!
Great weapons! Your conquest!

-- 2000
Ilorin

8.   THE COLD MOONS

Sometimes we stumble through the Cold Moons,
And dragged along by nature's tunes,
Only to halt and lay still upon life's pleasant lawn,
When it is born, a new and gentle dawn.

Sometimes when bathed in ocean of freezing snow,
Our world silently will become low.
Life usurped and hope opposed,
We carelessly long to surrender to fate, eternally reposed.

But when the cold moons slowly hide their sights,
Life once again will spring up in summer's splendoured
nights.
And then witness the night wind act like sharp metals,
Beheading beautiful roses by their long petals.

Spread and suspended across the twinkling sky,
Along with their soothing fragrance, above they ply.
Then a time to exult at life's gentle breeze,
Under the canopies of nightingale's trees.

Reminded that delights'n'dangers shoot upon a stalk,
We'll be showed what trials life thrust upon us in stuck.
During those time of voyages through the Cold Moons,
When we had no guts to break nature's tunes.

-- 2002
Lagos

9. DRIFTING THOUGHTS

Mind shifts…
Thought drifts…
That life's more beautiful is vanquished,
Cos' life'll soon be extinguished.

Mind shifts…
Thought drifts…
That now the heart kisses the moon,
Cos' Joy's slender body'll break too soon.

Mind shifts…
Thought drifts…
That today hails you with many commendations,
Cos' tomorrow'll soon trail you with more condemnations.

Mind shifts…
Thought drifts…
That you fall so in love today,
Cos' you'll soon hate after this day.

Mind shifts…
Thought drifts…

That all hopes're so high,
Cos' they'll later drop from the sky.

Mind shifts…
Thought drifts…
That life's so gloomy with sorrow,
Cos' you don't know what's at stake tomorrow.

Mind shifts…
Thought drifts…
The same way daylight drifts into the night,
And the night slowly to the broad daylight.

Thought drifts on and drifts…
Mind shifts on and shifts…
Cos' our mind's the ship we can't see,
Caught in the dancing intrigues of uncharted sea.

-- 26/8/05
12.00pm
Lagos

10. *MOON NIGHT*

What kind of a night is this?
What creature it is above the sky,
That stops to catch my attention?
What kind of a strange night is this?
Must this be to me a night of realization?
Oh! This night, when the creature is fully grown
Surrounded by beautiful gallant stars,
Struts his hour upon the earth,
To celebrate his majestic arrival
It is the night when total darkness cease to-prevail
The night when old tales are told
By the old lads to their young ones
This is a night of peace for the older folks
As they lie down on their bed-chair
To enjoy the chill of the ocean breeze
This is a night of love and unity for the children
It is the moon-night, the night of the moon
When all the country siblings come together
To play, chant and dance in the moon-light
Till they finally retire to their beddings

-- 4/5/99
7.09pm
Lagos

11. DOXOLOGIES

When the birds ply 'n' cry in the sky
When the fishes dive 'n trickle in the sea
When the ants 'n' the dwellers of the soil
Burrow with joy, deep into the mystery of the underworld
When the trees stretch out their strength
Against the turbulent storms of the wilderness
And breathe out merciful breeze upon mortals
In the stillness of the night
When the beasts of forest too
Sparkle 'n' dance to the brightness of the day
When men chorus to the dazzling wonders of galaxies
Accompanied by regular trail of coasting night moon
To NATURE…they tender their Doxologies…Doxologies

-- 3/3/03
12.00pm
Lagos

12. TOMORROW

My friend! Know that tomorrow will never come to you
If you cease to rise up 'n' run after it too
For how can you be so dense?
To sit there all days on the fence
And always expect good morrow to come
The source of encumbrance for some
How? How then can heaven lift you out of your woods?
When you fail to turn around your moods
Remember my friend! The price's too cost to live on shadowed hope
When you've choices with what you can cope
So beware! Don't be hooked by time 'n' swallowed like a bream
Living 'n' sleeping in the shadow of a midsummer's night dream.

-- 5/4/02
5.07pm
Lagos

13. UNFINISHED TASK

Oh! Heavy task lay upon my head
I seek a peaceful path out of the dread
I sit upon my weary bones
Fighting against my soul's shady phones
To let me off a lonely place
That I be free of life's stressful race
I laboured through harsh sun and rain
Shall all my toils be left to rot away in vain?
What I started, a burden unmasks!
Now, I must go back and finish my task!

-- 23/10/04
6.30pm
Lagos

14. OUR LOVE

Let's make it work today
Now that the chances are before us
Cos this life's too short
To delay the love we can always give

Let's do it now 'n' not wait till morrow
For we might wake up then 'n' get hurt
When these chances might've been lost
And too late to give our Love

-- 29/11/03
6.30pm
Ilorin

15. *A PENITENT'S PRAYER*

Forgive! Have mercy upon me...O Lord!
For my doom now I fear by thy word
I know thy cautions always I defy
But do not my penitence deny

O Lord! I bow down before thy will
And now, tears have my eyes fill
My heart wails…trembles with shame
My stubbornness now myself deny and blame

The time I should not've thy boundary crossed
I snubbed! In earthly lust was I engrossed
Ah! All's vanity! My journey…now resilience
I am but only a mortal in penitence

Lord! If thou have mercy upon me
And let thy forgiveness be
I shall forever cease my penniless mortal's ills
And never again question whatever thy wills

You gave me life, sustenance and protection
Now I fervently seek thy redemption
From this stubborn ungrateful ignorant soul
Which've swept thy mercy beneath it's sole

O Lord! Forgive me; Let me be wise
Cover me from all worldly vice
Show me the way to offer my thanks
That I be placed among the grateful ranks

O Lord! I have done great wrongs
And wounded my soul with rotten prongs
If thou me not forgive and let thy mercy boom
I shall melt away to eternal doom

Forgive me…accept my penitence, O Lord!
I, like a tamed lion bow now to thy WORD
My futile journey's end…now resilience
I am but only a mortal in penitence.

-- 1/9/04
6.15am
Lagos

Epilogue

"No man is an Island, entire of itself…
any man's death diminishes me, because
I am involved with Mankind; and therefore
never send to know for whom the bell tolls;
It tolls for thee."
-- John Donne (1572-1631).